Bradwell's Pocket Walking Guides

Somerset

BRADWELL
BOOKS

Published by Bradwell Books
9 Orgreave Close Sheffield S13 9NP
Email: books@bradwellbooks.co.uk

The right of Sue Robinson to be identified as author of this work has been asserted by her in accordance with the Copyright, Design and Patents Act, 1988.

All rights reserved. No part of this publication may be reproduced, stored in a retrieval system or transmitted in any form or by any means, electronic, mechanical, photocopying, recording or otherwise without the prior permission of Bradwell Books.

British Library Cataloguing in Publication Data: a catalogue record for this book is available from the British Library.

1st Edition
ISBN: 9781910551912
Extracts edited by: Louise Maskill
Design, typesetting and mapping: Mark Titterton
Photograph credits: Front Cover - iStock
Print: Gomer Press, Llandysul, Ceredigion SA44 4JL

Maps contain Ordnance Survey data
© Crown copyright and database right 2017

CONTENTS

Fact File & Introduction			**p.5**
Walk 1	**Lorna Doone Valley**	3 miles	**p.6**
Walk 2	**Dunster Castle**	4 miles	**p.10**
Walk 3	**Glastonbury Tor**	2½ miles	**p.14**
Walk 4	**Brean Down**	3½ miles	**p.18**
Walk 5	**Bath**	4 miles	**p.22**
Walk 6	**Stanton Drew**	3¼ miles	**p.28**
Walk 7	**East Quantoxhead**	3 miles	**p.32**
Walk 8	**King Alfred's Tower**	4 miles	**p.36**
Walk 9	**Martock**	3¾ miles	**p.40**
Walk 8	**Wookey Hole**	6 miles	**p.44**

FACT FILE & INTRODUCTION

FACT FILE

The information in the walk descriptions is produced in good faith, and should be adequate to get you from start to finish, but it is always advisable to take a relevant Ordnance Survey map with you. The correct maps for each walk are recommended in 'The Essentials' sections – OS Explorer maps are highly detailed maps of a relatively small area (1:25,000 scale, 4cm on the map equals 1km on the ground), while the OS Landranger series are less detailed (1:50,000 scale, 2cm on the map equals 1km on the ground) but show a larger area per map. For these walks the Landranger maps are adequate, but the Explorer maps are more precise – the choice is yours.

All the walks in this book follow rights of way or paths open to the public, with occasional roadside paths (take care when crossing roads). The walks should be suitable for most people, especially families, ranging in length from around 2½ to 6 miles. They are graded and described in 'The Essentials' sections to help you select the most appropriate walk for your party. Walking boots are recommended for all walks, with plenty of insulating layers of clothing and a waterproof jacket and overtrousers if indicated by the weather forecast.

Locations for purchasing refreshments are suggested in 'The Essentials' sections, but are usually located at the start and end points of the walks, so packing a drink and a snack for your walk is advisable. Take advantage of public toilets where available!

By law, dogs must be kept on a lead wherever there is livestock, as well as in moorland areas during nesting season and where sheep roam freely. They should also be on a lead if they are likely to be a nuisance to other walkers or cyclists, and certainly when crossing roads. **You should be sure that your dog can manage to get over stiles before you set off on any of these walks; see 'Route' in 'The Essentials' to check whether there are any stiles on the walk you would like to undertake.**

Bradwell Books and the author have made all reasonable efforts to ensure that the details are correct at the time of publication. Bradwell Books and the author cannot accept responsibility for any changes that have taken place subsequent to the book being published. It is the responsibility of individuals undertaking any of the walks listed in this book to exercise due care and consideration for their own health and wellbeing and that of others in their party. The walks in this book are not especially strenuous, but individuals taking part should ensure that they are fit and well before setting off.

INTRODUCTION

Somerset is a county of contrasts. It contains three Areas of Outstanding Natural Beauty in the rolling hills of the Quantocks, the Mendips and the Blackdowns, and two thirds of the Exmoor National Park is located in the county, offering the visitor a wide variety of wonderful scenery with moors, river valleys and the beautiful coastline facing South Wales.

In ancient times Somerset was known as "the land of summer" – because of the extensive autumn and winter flooding which made the lower lands of the Somerset Levels uninhabitable except in the summer months. Prehistoric farmers worked on the hills during the winter and grazed their animals on the lush grass on the Levels during the summer. The wetlands of the Somerset Levels, which are predominantly below sea level and are still subject to flooding, are rich in flora and fauna, and in the winter are visited by many wading birds.

The Somerset coastline offers everything from cliff-top walks to miles of sandy beaches and offshore islands. There are small coastal villages and Victorian resort towns with elegant piers, as well as a number of holiday parks and resorts along the coastline.

Taunton is the largest town in Somerset and is the administrative centre for the county. With evidence of settlement in the area going back around three thousand years, the town is steeped in history and contains many old and beautiful buildings. The Romans traded in lead, which they found in the Mendip Hills, developing the city of Bath as a famous spa resort, while many of the smaller towns were established on the cloth and wool industry in medieval times. There are many ruined castles and impressive early manor houses, together with the well-known Georgian grandeur of Bath.

Agriculture and food and drink production are two of the major economic drivers in the area; who hasn't heard of Somerset cider? However, there have been heavier industrial activities in the county too, with a history of quarrying and textile manufacture. These days tourism is a valuable contributor, and rightly so – Somerset is a beautiful county well worth the exploring.

1. LORNA DOONE VALLEY

THE ESSENTIALS

Distance: 3 miles (5 km)

Route: Easy, level track with a gentle incline. Several gates, no stiles

Time: Approx. 1½ hours

Terrain: Wide stony and grass tracks, field paths

Starting Point: Lorna Doone Farm car park, Malmsmead. Grid ref SS 791 477, postcode EX35 6NU

Parking: Lorna Doone Farm car park, as above

Food and Toilets: Café Deli at Lorna Doone Farm. Public toilets in the car park

Maps: OS Explorer 9 (Exmoor); OS Landranger 180 (Barnstaple and Ilfracombe), 181 (Minehead and Brendon Hills)

INTRODUCTION

This beautiful walk takes you along the Doone Valley and Badgworthy Water, with a gentle climb out of the valley providing wonderful views of the surrounding area, and then on to Oare Church. The walk uses wide stony tracks and paths across fields; there are no stiles, but it may be muddy in wet weather.

The village of Oare is situated on the border of Somerset and Devon in the Exmoor National Park. It is said that Lorna Doone Valley and Badgworthy Water are where the author R.D. Blackmore located, and was inspired to write, his novel *Lorna Doone*, a romantic tale about two rival families who lived on the moor. Blackmore, who lived in London, used to come and stay with his grandfather who was the Rector of Oare, and who would tell him stories of the families who lived locally.

Oare Church of St Mary's has been a parish church for at least eight hundred years. In R.D. Blackmore's novel, Lorna is due to be married to John Ridd in this church, but she is shot by Carver Doone through a small window at the end of the church. Luckily Lorna survives the shooting and goes on to marry John Ridd at a later date.

Exmoor National Park is small and compact, with contrasting beautiful landscapes; it is ideal for families to tour and explore. Exmoor offers the visitor both moors and wooded valleys, as well as a magnificent coastline bordering the Bristol Channel. Two thirds of the National Park is in Somerset and one third in Devon.

1. LORNA DOONE VALLEY WALK

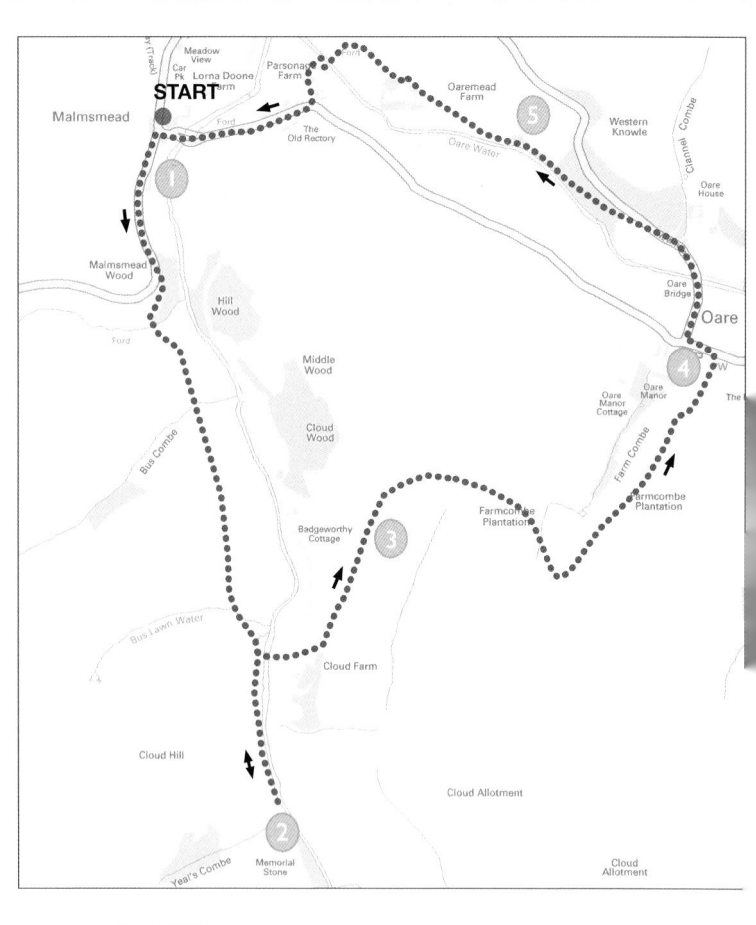

ROUTE

1. Leave the car park heading towards Lorna Doone Farm and the shop. Take the road to your right following the sign directing you to 'Lane leading to Public Footpath Doone Valley'. Follow this uphill to where the road curves right, and go straight on through a gate to the left.

BRADWELL'S POCKET WALKING GUIDE

2. Continue to follow the track for approximately 1 mile with Badgworthy Water on your left until you reach a memorial stone for R.D. Blackmore. Turn and retrace your steps back along the track, with the river now on your right, until you reach a wooden bridge. Cross the river and enter a field, the camping site at Cloud Farm. Continue straight ahead towards a red phonebox and a wooden signpost.

3. Follow the hard track bearing left towards the farm buildings, and continue into and through the farm. Continue through a metal farm gate and follow the track ahead, up towards another gate. Go through the gate, following a grassy track as it bears uphill and to the right. At the top of the hill, go through another gate and continue ahead on a grass track, following it as it bears to the right.

4. Go through another gate and follow the track as it bears left, keeping to the left down the slope to another gate. Go through and continue down the grass track, with the fence on your left, to reach a gate and road.

5. Turn left on the road and the entrance to Oare Church will be on your left. After visiting the church, turn left back onto the road and then immediately right (signposted Lynmouth/Porlock), continuing along the road which crosses the bridge over Oare Water. As the road curves left follow the footpath sign on your left, marked Malmsmead.

6. Go through the gate and follow the grass track across a field to another gate. Continue through a series of gates, passing Oaremead Farm on your left. At the last gate by a wooden signpost, turn left along a track between two hedges to meet Oare Water. Turn right and cross a footbridge. Continue up the track to pass through a gate and ahead to the road, where you turn right. The road then takes you past the entrance to Cloud Farm and back to Lorna Doone Farm.

2. DUNSTER CASTLE

THE ESSENTIALS

Distance: 4 miles (6.5 km)

Route: Undulating with one main uphill climb. Several gates, no stiles

Time: Approx. 2 hours

Terrain: Pavements, tracks ,open countryside which may be muddy

Starting Point: Car park at Gallox Bridge.
Grid ref SS 989 432, postcode TA24 6SR

Parking: Pay and display car park via Park Street at Gallox Bridge, as above

Food and Toilets: Various restaurants in the village. Public toilets in the village

Maps: OS Explorer 9 (Exmoor);
OS Landranger 181 (Minehead and Brendon Hills)

INTRODUCTION

Bat's Castle is an Iron Age hillfort on the summit of a 692ft (210m) hill, with spectacular 360-degree panoramas of Exmoor and the coast. The route of this walk takes you through Dunster Deer Park along field paths and stony tracks with some uphill climbs. When wet the fields can be muddy.

Dunster is situated in the Exmoor National Park, which has a landscape of great variety and covers 267 square miles (692 square kilometres) of Somerset and Devon. The magnificent Dunster Castle is a former motte and bailey castle, now a country house. It stands at the top of a steep hill called the Tor, and has been fortified since the late Anglo-Saxon period. In the eleventh

BRADWELL'S POCKET WALKING GUIDE

century William de Mohun constructed a timber castle on the site as part of the pacification of Somerset. A stone shell keep was built on the motte by the start of the twelfth century, and at the end of the fourteenth century the castle was sold to the Luttrell family, who continued to occupy the property until the late twentieth century.

The walk is in the Dunster Forest Crown Estate. The lands belonging to the castle were sold to the Crown in 1950, and cover over 9,000 acres. The land consists of the most beautiful countryside with forests, woodlands heaths and agricultural land. In 1976 the castle and all its remaining land were given to the National Trust, and it is open to visitors.

There are numerous paths and trails across the estate. Bat's Castle is one of the larger Iron Age hillforts on Exmoor. It is unusual as it has a ditched causeway projecting outwards from the entrance. There are a number of outlying ditches to the south-east, which may have been dug when the fort was used as a camp in the Civil War. On reaching the fort you will be amazed by the magnificent views of the Bristol Channel, Minehead, and even as far as the Welsh Coast on a clear day.

The medieval Deer Park was landscaped for the Luttrell family in 1755 to enhance the castle grounds. The park supplied venison and other game for the castle. Fallow deer can still be found in the area, but they are not confined to the park boundaries.

2. DUNSTER CASTLE WALK

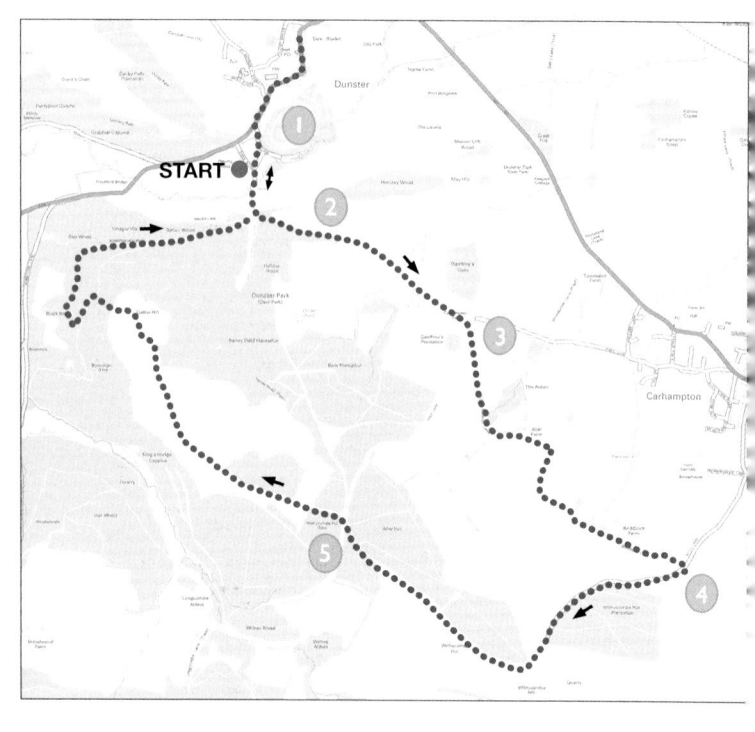

ROUTE

1. From the car park, turn left and walk between the cottages towards Gallox Bridge. Cross the bridge and continue ahead in the direction of Dunster Forest Crown Estate, passing a thatched cottage on your right.

2. On reaching the information board go through the kissing gate and follow the signpost reading 'Carhampton 1 mile'. Slowly ascend through the deer park, and after a few hundred metres join a fence line on your left. Continue uphill, and then drop down to pass through a hunting gate. Continue to follow

BRADWELL'S POCKET WALKING GUIDE

the fence line to the brow of the hill, to pass through a gate and immediately reach Park Lane (a track).

3. Take the footpath across the lane and go over a stile into a field. Cross diagonally, aiming for the gap in the far hedge, to the right of a barn at Aller Farm. Follow the grassy track ahead between barns, and where the track bends sharp left, turn right through a gate into a field and then sharp left to walk with the hedge on your left. Pass through a gate and turn right to follow the hedge, passing through a further gate, and then bear left to a track which takes you through several gates and passes through the farmyard of Briddicott Farm.

4. Reach a road in front of the farmhouse, and where it bends sharp left, continue ahead, following a track between barns and then between hedges. Join Hill Lane (a track) at a T-junction and turn right, walking steadily uphill until you reach a cattle grid. Keep on uphill into more open country, and join another track coming in from your left. This is the Macmillan Way West; you will see a signpost to Dunster (2.5 miles). Past the signpost, follow the track over the top of Withycombe Hill, keeping to the edge of the conifer plantation to your right.

5. Arrive at a gate into the plantation, continue ahead, and almost immediately you reach a Y-junction. Take the right fork to come to a major path junction at Withycombe Hill Gate. Here, turn left through the large gate, following the bridleway to Dunster. Continue uphill (ignoring a footpath to Dunster on the right) past Bat's Castle, and then start to descend. Follow the Bat's Castle Circuit signposts, which will take you back to Gallox Bridge and the car park.

3. GLASTONBURY TOR

THE ESSENTIALS

Distance: 2½ miles (4 km)

Route: Medium; steep climb to the top of the Tor. Several gates, no stiles

Time: Approx. 1½ hours

Terrain: Pavements, concrete track up the Tor, steps, field paths

Starting Point: Glastonbury Abbey car park, Magdalene Street, Glastonbury. **Grid ref** ST 499 388 **postcode** BA6 9EH

Parking: Paid-for parking at Glastonbury Abbey car park, as above

Food and Toilets: Various restaurants and cafés in town. Public toilets in the Abbey car park and in the town

Maps: OS Explorer 141 (Cheddar Gorge and Mendip Hills West); **OS Landranger** 112 (Weston-super-Mare)

INTRODUCTION

The mystical town of Glastonbury is situated on the Somerset Levels 23 miles (35 kilometres) from Bristol. It is noted for its myths and legends as well as the famous Glastonbury Festival, although the Festival site is actually situated a few miles from Glastonbury at a small village called Pilton.

Glastonbury Abbey was one of the richest and grandest abbeys in England. The Abbey was founded in the seventh century by the Saxon king Ine of Wessex. When the Normans invaded England and conquered the Saxons they took over the Abbey and added additional buildings, and it became the richest monastery in England. It is said that King Arthur and Queen Guinevere are buried here. The abbots of the monastery lived in great splendour, but during the time of Henry VIII and the dissolution of the monasteries Glastonbury Abbey and all its land and properties were sold off or leased to new lay occupiers.

Over the centuries many pilgrims have visited Glastonbury. The most famous is reported to have been Joseph of Arimathea, the uncle of Jesus, who brought with him the Holy Grail, the cup that was used by Christ at the Last Supper. It is said that Joseph landed in Avalon at Wearyall Hill and stuck his staff into the ground. Overnight it took root and grew into what we know today as the famous Glastonbury Thorn. This thorn tree flowers at Christmas, and a sprig is cut each year and sent to the Queen. Joseph hid the Holy Grail for safekeeping, burying it below the Tor. A spring emerged at the site, and the water which flows from it is said to give eternal youth. This is the Chalice Well, which you will pass on your walk to the Tor.

Glastonbury Tor is known as one of the most spiritual sites in the country. It was a significant site to the pre-Christian pagans, and it is still celebrated today by Christian pilgrims. Many hundreds of years ago it was an island, since much of the Somerset Levels were under water. The medieval church of St Michael stood until 1275, when it was destroyed by an earthquake. A new church was built in the fourteenth century and stood here until the dissolution of the monasteries in 1539, when the Tor became a place of execution. Today it is managed by the National Trust.

3. GLASTONBURY TOR WALK

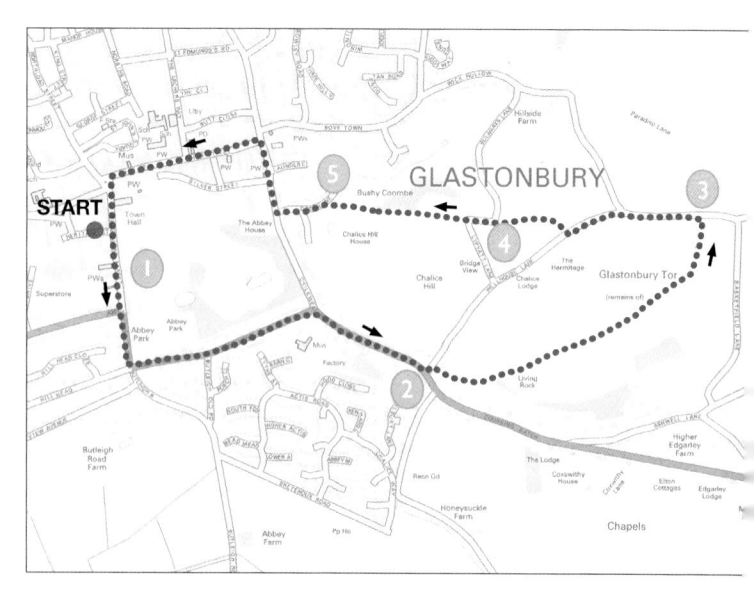

ROUTE

1. Leave the car park, turn left and walk ahead the pavement up Fishers Hill, passing the Catholic Church on your right. Follow the pavement around to the left, passing Somerset Rural Life Museum on your right, until you reach a roundabout. Cross the road with care and turn right; you are now on Chilkwell Street. Continue ahead, passing old cottages on your left and the Rifleman Pub on your right, to reach the Chalice Well and Gardens on your left. A short distance after the Chalice Well, at Wellhouse Lane, turn left and almost immediately right again.

2. Continue ahead to reach a kissing gate and the entrance to Glastonbury Tor. Follow the steep zig-zag footpath to the top of the Tor and St Michael's Tower. After spending some

BRADWELL'S POCKET WALKING GUIDE

time at the top of the Tor, descend by the shorter concrete footpath which starts on the right-hand side of St Michael's Tower and continues down to two kissing gates and the road.

3. On reaching the road turn left and continue ahead, ignoring the road to the right, until you reach a kissing gate in the hedge on your right signposted Dod Lane. Go through the gate and across a field to a further kissing gate, and continue ahead along a path between two hedges to reach a road. Do not follow it left, but go straight ahead.

4. Pass through a metal kissing gate with views over the town of Glastonbury. Follow a grassy path down to another kissing gate. After going through the gate and onto the road, note the Tibetan Prayer Wheels on your left. The prayer wheels are full of thousands of prayers, and turning the wheels in a clockwise direction sends the prayers out into the world.

5. Continue ahead to meet the main road. Turn right and then cross the road and turn right and then left into Silver Street. Continue along this road, passing a car park on your left and following the road as it curves around to right; you then enter the High Street opposite the parish church of St John. Turn left on reaching the High Street and walk beside the shops, following the pavement around to the left, passing the Town Hall on your left and then back to the car park.

4. BREAN DOWN

THE ESSENTIALS

Distance: 3½ miles (5.5 km)

Route: Medium; steep climb initially. No stiles

Time: Approx. 1¾ hours

Terrain: Grassy track and rough road

Starting Point: National Trust car park, Brean Down. Grid ref ST 296 585, postcode TA8 2RS

Parking: National Trust car park as above (charge for non-NT members)

Food and Toilets: Bird Garden Café. No public toilets on the route

Maps: OS Explorer 153 (Weston-super-Mare); OS Landranger 182 (Weston-super-Mare)

INTRODUCTION

The village of Brean lies on the shore of the Somerset coast alongside the beach. Brean Down is one of the most dramatic landmarks on the Somerset coastline, and offers an opportunity for lovely walks. In Brean village and along the coast there are a number of holiday and leisure parks. Brean Down is a massive finger of limestone escarpment which juts into the Bristol Channel and is the continuation of the Mendip Hills. Steep Holm and Flat Holm, which can be seen out in the Channel from the top of the ridge, are the true end of the Mendip Hills. The Down stands 320 feet (97m) high and the views from the top are truly spectacular, looking out over the Bristol Channel towards South Wales and over the Somerset Levels and the stunning coastline.

The fort at the end of the peninsula was built in the 1860s as part of a grand scheme of defences devised to see off the threat of a

French invasion. Such fortifications have since become known as Palmerston's Follies, because they became obsolete within just a few years of being built as a result of large-scale improvements in naval gunnery. The fort was home to three 7-inch rifled muzzle-loading guns. Working with similar batteries on the Welsh coast and on the islands of Steep Holm and Flat Holm, the fort served to protect the city of Bristol from raiders navigating up the Severn Estuary. The fort was destroyed in 1900 by a rogue artilleryman who discharged his weapon down a ventilation shaft. The site was rendered unusable and remained out of use until World War II. These days it is rich in wildlife, history and archaeology, and is a Site of Special Scientific Interest.

4. BREAN DOWN WALK

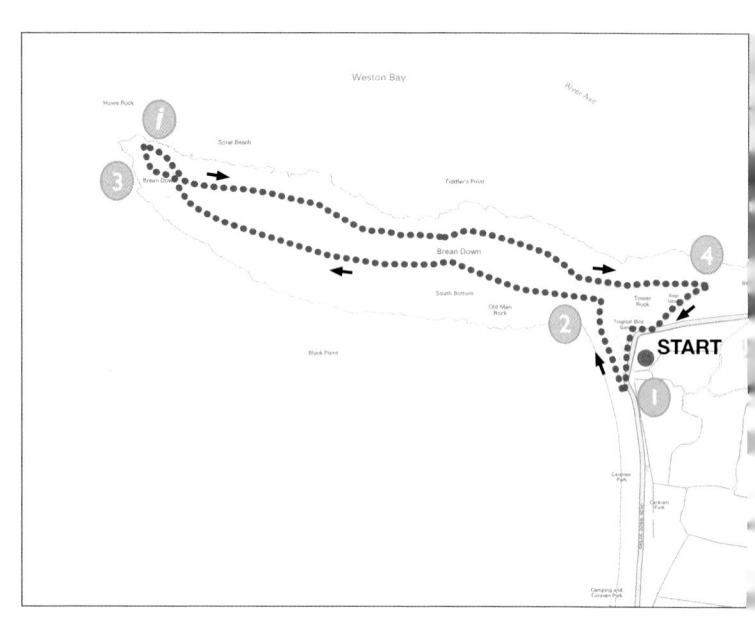

ROUTE

1. Leave the National Trust car park to your right and walk along the stony road towards the Bird Gardens. Keeping to the left of the café, follow the track towards the steps and the headland which can be seen ahead of you. Climb the steps to the top of the limestone escarpment. It is a steep climb, so take your time and absorb the panoramic views of the Somerset Levels, the Bristol Channel and, on a good day, the Welsh coast.

2. At the top of the headland, turn left and head westward along the worn grassy path climbing gently to the highest point of the Down. En route you will pass the remains of both an old Roman temple and ancient field systems. You

BRADWELL'S POCKET WALKING GUIDE

will reach a trig point, where you should make another stop to admire the wonderful view of Flat Holm and Steep Holm ahead of you, and south to Hinkley nuclear power station and beyond to Exmoor.

3. Continue to the end of the peninsula, where you will find the extensive fortifications of Brean Down Fort. Entry to the old fortifications is free and there are a number of information boards. You reach the site by crossing a small bridge to the right of the buildings.

4. After visiting the fort, return by crossing the small bridge and keeping slightly left, heading along the old tarmac road which used to bring men and munitions to the fort. Continue to follow the road, passing World War II gun emplacements and with wonderful views of Weston-super-Mare and the River Axe estuary on your left. The track then bears around to your right and descends gently to a gate. Go through the gate and, keeping right, follow the track back to the car park.

5. BATH

THE ESSENTIALS

Distance: 4 miles (6.5 km)

Route: Easy, small inclines, some steps. No stiles

Time: Approx. 2 hours

Terrain: Surfaced paths, canal towpaths, gravel path

Starting Point: Bath Abbey. Grid ref ST 750 647; postcode BA1 1LT

Parking: Pay and display at SouthGate car park (postcode BA1 1TP) or park and ride from Lansdown (north of Bath), Newbridge (west of Bath) or Odd Down (south of Bath)

Food and Toilets: Restaurants and cafés in Bath centre. Several public toilets in the city

Maps: OS Explorer 155 (Bristol and Bath); OS Landranger 172 (Bristol and Bath)

INTRODUCTION

The City of Bath was designated as a World Heritage Site in 1987 and is a major centre for tourism. Founded by the Romans as a thermal spa, Bath also became an important centre of the wool industry in the Middle Ages. Bath has over five thousand listed buildings, and a large part of the city is a conservation area. The beautiful Georgian buildings built out of locally quarried Bath Stone remind us that the city was, and still is, a very important spa and cultural centre. Bath has a number of public parks, the largest being the Royal Victoria Park overlooked by the spectacular Royal Crescent, one of the many Georgian terraces which can be found in the city.

Bath is located on the River Avon and is connected to Bristol and the sea by this river. The Kennet and Avon Canal was built in

1810 to join the Avon to the River Thames and London. The canal was closed for many years but has been restored and is now used for boating, walking and cycling, and is also important for wildlife conservation.

This interesting walk takes you from the centre of Bath through the Georgian streets, along the Kennet and Avon Canal and the River Avon. It visits the Botanical Gardens and passes the well-known Royal Crescent, the Circus, the Pump Room and the Roman Baths. If you would also like a little retail therapy the walk takes you through the main shopping area and its many arcades. The walk is mostly on surfaced paths and the canal towpath.

5. BATH WALK

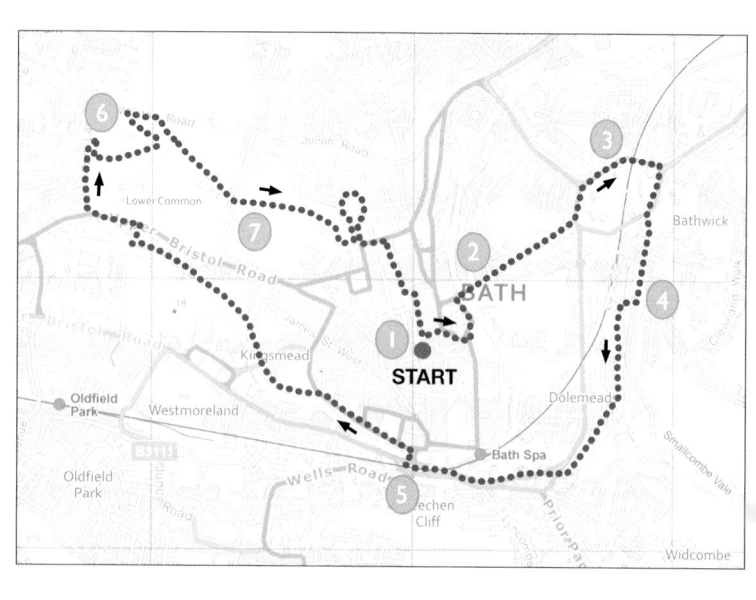

ROUTE

1. Facing Bath Abbey with the Pump Room on your right, make your way across the square to the corner of York Street. Walk along York Street to the road and the river. Cross the road and go left, following the stone wall to your right to reach Pulteney Bridge.

2. Cross Pulteney Bridge with shops on either side; continue ahead towards the Holburne Museum. Cross the road and go left, passing the museum entrance on your right, and at the corner turn right into Sydney Gardens.

3. Continue ahead along a tarmac path through the gardens, crossing two bridges. Bearing slightly right, follow the path alongside the tennis courts and around to the right to reach

the park entrance and road. Cross the road and go right; ignore Sham Castle Lane to your left, but take the adjacent waymarked track to the canal.

4. Keeping left, follow the towpath until you reach a road. Cross the road and go right, and at the end of the wall turn sharp left and go down steps to the canal again. Turn right and continue along the towpath, passing several locks to reach a road and then a second road. Here, go left along a walkway over the lock and left down steps to the canal. The canal is now on your right; follow the path until you reach the end of the canal and its confluence with the River Avon. Cross the road and follow the walkway beside the river, walking under two metal bridges until you reach a pedestrian footbridge. Cross and turn left, cross a dual carriageway, and continue along the footpath until you reach a track on your left leading down to the river and the cycle/footpath.

5. Continue to follow the footpath under several bridges. After the suspension bridge continue ahead, and just before a further girder bridge take the narrow path right onto Midland Road. Turn right, walk to the busy road and cross with care, turning left and continuing to the corner of Park Lane. Turn right and walk up the hill, then turn right through a gap in the wall into the open park. Cross the road and go left; ahead you will see metal gates into the Botanic Gardens.

continued on page 26

5. BATH WALK

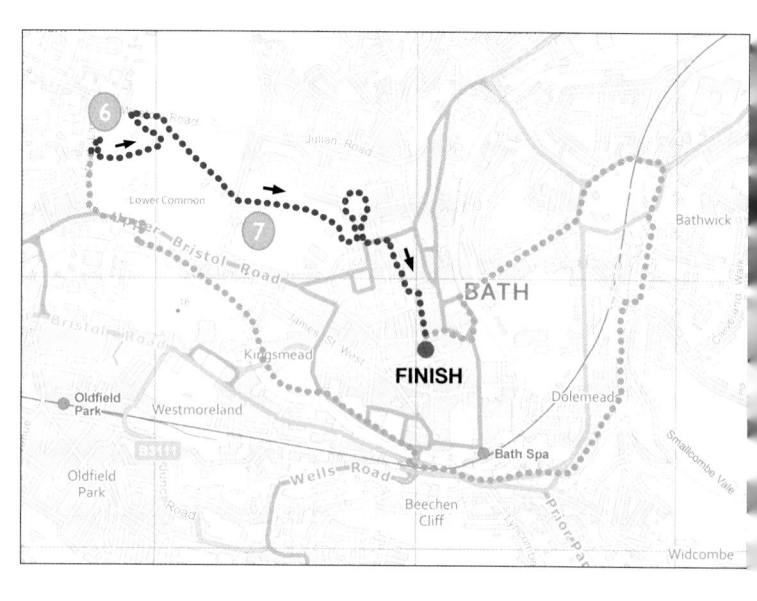

6. Enter the Botanic Gardens, go right and follow one of many paths to a pond. Pass around the pond, and near the Minerva Temple exit the gardens through metal gates onto the road. Cross the road, go right and follow the path a short distance. Across the road to your right you will see a fingerpost and a gravel track which goes diagonally across the open park. Follow this path until you reach a road; opposite is a lane marked 'no entry'. Follow the lane until you reach a road. Cross the road and follow the tarmac path through bollards and across the park in front of the Royal Crescent. On reaching a fingerpost on your right, turn left towards the Royal Crescent and then right at the road junction, following the road into the Circus.

26

BRADWELL'S POCKET WALKING GUIDE

7. Keeping left of the Circus, take the first exit left into Bennett Street. After a short distance turn right, passing the Assembly Rooms and Costume Museum on your left, and continue down the narrow street. At a T-junction turn right and follow the street around to your left before reaching George Street. Go left and cross the road to enter Milsom Street on your right. Continue ahead through the shopping area along Milsom Street, Burton Street, Union Street and Stall Street. The Abbey Churchyard is on your left through pillars.

6. STANTON DREW

THE ESSENTIALS

Distance: 3¼ miles (5 km)

Route: Easy, one short slope, several gates and no stiles

Time: Approx. 1¼ hours

Terrain: Field paths, may be muddy

Starting Point: Stanton Drew stone circle.
Grid ref ST 597 632; postcode BS39 4EW

Parking: Free parking adjacent to The Cove (the Druids Arms), postcode BS39 4EJ

Food and Toilets: Food at inns in Stanton Drew and Pensford. No public toilets on route

Maps: OS Explorer 155 (Bristol and Bath); OS Landranger 172 (Bristol and Bath)

INTRODUCTION

This easy walk starts at the Stanton Drew Stone Circle and takes you beside the River Chew, along a beautiful valley towards the village of Pensford. Before reaching Pensford you will see a magnificent viaduct and you will then return from Pensford back along the river to Stanton Drew.

Located 6 miles (10 kilometres) south of Bristol, Stanton Drew is very much a country village, with active farming and a traditional community. The village is most famous for its prehistoric stone circles, the largest being the Great Circle, a henge monument which is the second largest stone circle in Britain (after Avebury). The circle is 370 feet (113m) in diameter and probably originally contained 30 stones, of which 27 survive today. Also within the village, in the garden of the village pub, is another group of three large stones called The Cove, which was once part of the larger stone circle. The Stanton Drew stone circles are in the care of English Heritage but lie on private land, accessible on payment of a £1.00 entrance fee via an honesty box.

Pensford is a ribbon village alongside the A37 road. It has been identified as being of special architectural and historic interest and was designated as a Conservation Area in May 1988. During the fourteenth to sixteenth centuries Pensford was a textiles centre based on local wool, and during the nineteenth and twentieth centuries the main industry was coal mining, with Pensford and the surrounding area forming a major part of the Somerset coalfield. The magnificent railway viaduct, built of local stone, opened in 1873 to carry the Bristol and North Somerset Railway over the valley of the River Chew. The Pensford Viaduct is no longer used as a railway line, and since 1984 it has been Grade II listed. St Thomas à Becket Church dates from the fourteenth century, although only the tower remains from that date.

The River Chew rises at Chewton Mendip and flows for 17 miles (27 kilometres) along the beautiful Chew Valley before joining the River Avon at Keynsham. The River Chew has been dammed at Litton and Chew Stoke to form three reservoirs, providing drinking water to the Bristol Water region. The largest of these is Chew Valley Lake, known worldwide for fly fishing and one of the most important sites in the country for wintering wildfowl.

6. STANTON DREW WALK

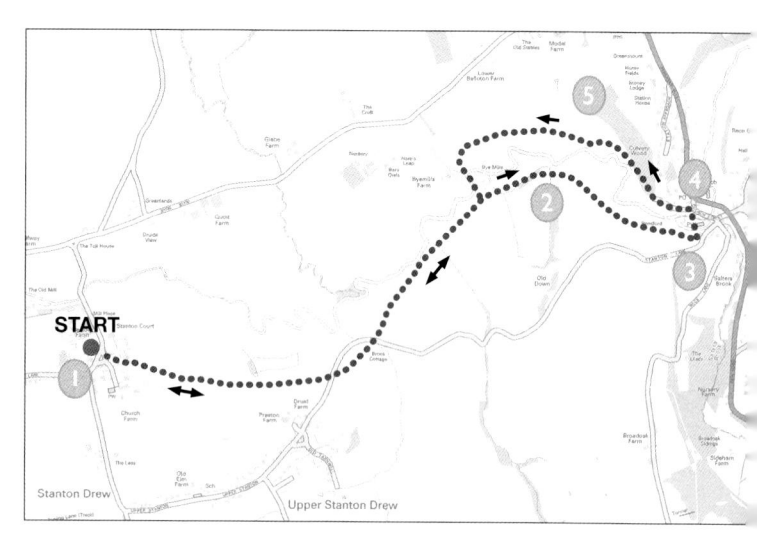

ROUTE

1. With your back to the car park, turn right and walk past the Druids Arms. Take the first turning right, following this road to reach a kissing gate and sign to Stone Circles. Through the gate, bear right to join a tarmac track towards farm buildings. Follow this track through several gates to a sewage works. Go through a gate right of the sewage works and continue across the field to a kissing gate in the hedge.

2. Follow the field path with the hedge on your left, and then bear right at the second telegraph pole to a gate and road. Cross the road and follow a short track up to a gate, then follow the field path along the edge of the field to a further gate and road. Cross the road and go through a kissing gate next to a fingerpost. Continue ahead across a field to a further gate; go through and head down towards the river.

BRADWELL'S POCKET WALKING GUIDE

Follow the riverbank to the lower gate next to the river and on towards the weir and mill buildings. On reaching the weir go through a wooden kissing gate onto a track and continue ahead, passing Byemills, a former iron and copper battery mill.

3. Through the next kissing gate, follow the path across the field to a kissing gate on your right, leading to an uphill path and wooden steps to open ground. Follow the path towards the viaduct over a small bridge.

4. As you pass under the viaduct take the path to the left to a very old bridge and weir. Cross the bridge and keep left, entering an area with a garage workshop. Follow around to your right between buildings to a T-junction. Turn left and immediately left again, following a footpath sign back uphill towards the viaduct.

5. On the brow of the hill, pass through a gate to enter Culvery Woods. Follow the wide track ahead towards a kissing gate. Go through and follow the path with the river on your left, to a gate by the river. Go through and continue ahead across a field to another gate in the hedge. Go through, over a small bridge and through another gate, then across the field to the lower kissing gate in the hedge corner. Go through this gate and across a field to another gate, and on to a further gate. Enter a small field and walk towards the houses, gate and road.

6. At the road, turn left and continue ahead between houses and back to Byemills weir. Cross the bridge and weir and turn right through a kissing gate. Retrace your steps back to the start, keeping the river on your right and following the same route as your outward journey.

7. EAST QUANTOXHEAD

THE ESSENTIALS

Distance: 3 miles (5 km)

Route: Easy, one slight uphill climb. No stiles

Time: Approx 1½ hours

Terrain: Tracks, field paths and cliff tops

Starting Point: Court House car park, East Quantoxhead. Grid ref ST 137 435, postcode TA5 1EJ

Parking: Small charge for parking at Court House car park, as above

Food and Toilets: Café at the Chantry, Kilve. No public toilets on route

Maps: OS Explorer 140 (Quantock Hills and Bridgewater); OS Landranger 181 (Minehead and Brenden Hills)

INTRODUCTION

This gentle walk takes you across open countryside and along a beautiful coastal path with wonderful views over the Bristol Channel, starting from the quiet village of East Quantockhead. There are opportunities to go fossil hunting on the beach at Kilve and visit two very interesting churches at Kilve and East Quantoxhead.

The Quantock Hills is a range of hills west of Bridgwater in Somerset. The range runs from the Vale of Taunton Deane in the south for about 15 miles (25 kilometres) to the north-west, ending at East Quantoxhead and West Quantoxhead on the coast of the Bristol Channel. The hills were England's first Area of Outstanding Natural Beauty.

East Quantock village appears to be caught in a time capsule, with its exquisite manor house, thatched cottages, medieval barns, its own duck pond and an old mill building. The manor house, known as the Court House, has been the home of the Luttrell family for seven and a half centuries. The small church of St Mary's lies close to the manor house wall, and contains some fantastic woodcarvings. The church was built of locally quarried grey lias and granite in its present position because of the risk of flooding in former times. It has a close association with the Luttrell family, containing the sixteenth century tomb of Sir Hugh Luttrell.

Kilve lies at the northern end of the Quantocks and is a picturesque village consisting of three settlements. Here you will find the ruins of the old Chantry, founded in 1329 and once used for storing barrels of spirits smuggled into Kilve Pill. The beach is a Site of Special Scientific Interest and a favourite haunt of geologists with its spectacular rock formations and fossils. Kilve also contains the remains of a red-brick retort built in 1924 after the shale in the cliffs was found to be rich in oil. The Shaline Company was founded in 1924 to exploit these strata, but was unable to raise sufficient capital. The company's retort house is thought to be the first structure erected for the conversion of shale to oil, and is all that remains of the anticipated Somerset oil boom.

7. EAST QUANTOXHEAD WALK

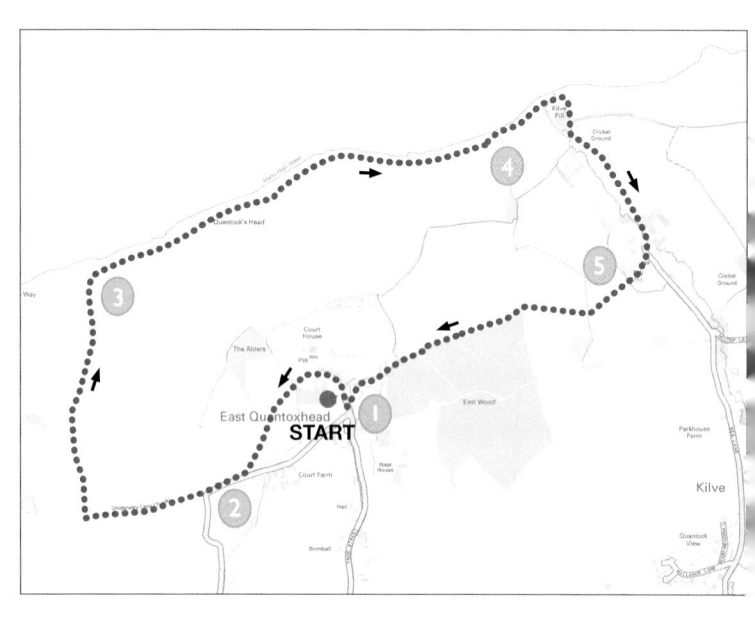

ROUTE

1. The walk starts from East Quantoxhead village at the Court House car park. Walk across the car park towards the church and the kissing gate. Go through the gate and follow a path that bends left towards a farm gate. You may wish to visit St Mary's Church at this point. Continue across the field to a further farm gate and road. Turn right on the road, and where it bends to the left take the grassy lane to the right.

2. Climb steadily up the lane to reach a kissing gate and farm gate on your right. Go through the gate and follow the permissive field path with the hedge on your right. Continue to follow the field path over two further fields and through two more kissing gates down to the clifftop.

3. The open clifftop path continues down towards a dip with a ruined lime kiln on your right. Here you bear right to cross the dip and then bear left to follow the clifftop path. Continue with a wire fence on your right, with the old Tudor Court House also in view. You will reach a kissing gate which takes you to a tarmac path, an open grassy area and Kilve beach.

4. Continue along the tarmac path towards a redbrick chimney, an old oil retort house used for oil distillation. Follow the path through the Kilve car park and along the road past the old Chantry to the Church of the Virgin Mary on your right.

5. Go through the church lychgate and keep to the left of the church to a kissing gate. Go through the gate and follow the farm track ahead, crossing a small bridge by a stream and across three fields to a kissing gate and farm gate. You are now on a stony track which bears right and left and takes you back into the village of East Quantoxhead by the village pond, arriving back at the Court House car park.

8. KING ALFRED'S TOWER

THE ESSENTIALS

Distance: 4 miles (6.5 km)

Route: Easy, small undulations. Several gates, no stiles

Time: Approx. 2 hours

Terrain: Forest track and field paths

Starting Point: King Alfred's Tower, Kingsettle Hill, South Brewham. **Grid ref** ST 745 350; **postcode** BA10 0LB

Parking: At King Alfred's Tower, on minor road off the B3092 from Frome as above.

Food and Toilets: National Trust Restaurant, Spread Eagle Inn. Public toilets: Stourhead Amenities

Maps: OS Explorer 142 (Mendip Hills East); OS Landranger 183 (Yeovil and Frome)

INTRODUCTION

This walk is on the Stourhead Estate and takes you from King Alfred's Tower along forest tracks and across open countryside. The route is mostly along the old carriage way used by the owners of Stourhead House in days gone by.

King Alfred's Tower was built in 1772 and stands on the border of the counties of Somerset, Wiltshire and Dorset; at 160 feet (49 metres) high it is reputedly one of the tallest follies in Britain. It stands on the point where King Alfred the Great is thought to have rallied his troops in AD 878 before the Battle of Edington. The tower is now owned by the National Trust and visitors are able to climb the two hundred and five steps to the top of the tower, from where there are wonderful views across the three counties.

BRADWELL'S POCKET WALKING GUIDE

The 2,650-acre Stourhead Estate is now owned and managed by the National Trust, and was given to the Trust in 1945 by the Hoare family. Stourhead House was one of the first country villas to be built in the new Palladian style and was designed by Colen Campbell for Henry Hoare I, who unfortunately died in the same year in which the house was completed. The famous gardens were designed by Henry Hoare II and laid out between 1741 and 1780 in a classical eighteenth century design set around a large lake, created by damming a small stream. Included in the garden are a number of temples inspired by scenes of the Grand Tour of Europe. On one hill overlooking the gardens there stands an obelisk and King Alfred's Tower, while on another hill a temple of Apollo provides a vantage point to survey the magnificent rhododendrons, water cascades and temples. The large medieval Bristol High Cross was moved from Bristol to the gardens. Among the hills surrounding the estate there are also two Iron Age hill forts.

8. KING ALFRED'S TOWER WALK

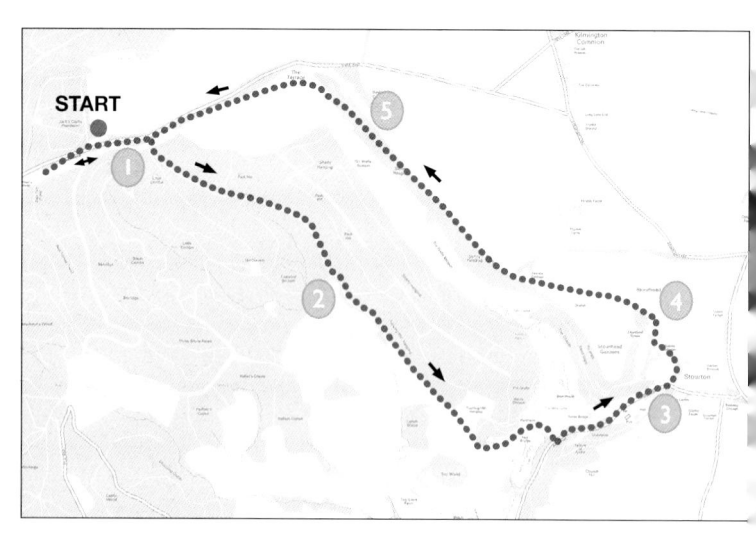

ROUTE

1. Leave the car park, cross the road and enter a grassy area. King Alfred's Tower is to your right. After visiting the Tower, retrace your steps and take the third track on the right, identified by a fingerpost sign. The track takes you downhill and undulates through the woods; continue on the main track, ignoring any left or right turns, until you reach a gate and stile.

2. Go through the gate and into the field and continue ahead, passing through a gate to a track; continue ahead in the direction of Turners Paddock. Pass through a further gate with a stile and follow a track through a field with Beech Cottage on your left. Wind your way down, passing a signpost for Stourton, to a further gate. Continue until you reach a road; turn left, passing under a rock arch.

BRADWELL'S POCKET WALKING GUIDE

3. You are now in the village of Stourton, with the entrance to the famous gardens on your left. Pass the parish church of St Peter and turn right into the courtyard of the Spread Eagle Inn. Cross the courtyard under the archway between shops. Follow the path ahead up towards the Stourhead reception area, but when the path bears right, go left to meet a road.

4. Cross the road and go through the ancient gateway, continuing along the driveway and passing in front of Stourhead House to a cattle grid and gate. Go through the gate, turning left to follow the "Carriage Way". Continue to follow this track, passing through a gate to the next field where you will see an obelisk. Continue along, passing through two gates with Terrace Lodge house on your right. You have now entered the Terrace; follow this walk for around half a mile (1 kilometre) to another gate.

5. Pass through the gate and follow the field as it bears left at the top. Continue along the ridge, passing through a gate, and then continue in the same direction, and after a further half-mile (1 kilometre) you will arrive back at King Alfred's Tower.

9. MARTOCK

THE ESSENTIALS

Distance: 3¾ miles (6 km)

Route: Easy, undulating route. Five stiles

Time: Approx. 2 hours

Terrain: Field paths, farm tracks, country roads

Starting Point: Martock Recreation Ground, Stoke Road, Martock. **Grid ref** ST 463 192; **postcode** TA12 6AF

Parking: Large car park at Martock Recreation Ground, as above

Food and Toilets: Various pubs and cafés, as well as public toilets, in Martock village

Maps: OS Explorer 129 (Yeovil);
OS Landranger 193 (Taunton and Lyme Regis)

INTRODUCTION

This easy, undulating walk takes you from the historic village of Martock, passing many beautiful buildings, across open countryside with wonderful views of South Petherton and the River Parrett Valley. The picturesque village of Martock is well worth exploring with its many blue plaque buildings, shops, pubs and cafés.

Martock, together with Hurst and Bower Hinton, forms a long village between the Rivers Isle and Parrett. It was once a centre of commerce and industry and is now a haven for arts, crafts and heritage. The name Martock comes from the Old English words "mart", meaning market, and "ac", meaning oak, and relate to an ancient oak tree on the spot now occupied by the Market House.

BRADWELL'S POCKET WALKING GUIDE

Martock's many attractive and historic buildings are constructed in stone from the nearby Ham Hill. This golden sedimentary Hamstone lends a mellow warmth to the buildings, some of which date back to the medieval period.

In the sixteenth and seventeenth centuries Martock enjoyed a period of great prosperity due to the fertile local soils and good farming practices. By the eighteenth and early nineteenth centuries it was the clothing and glove-making trades that created wealth for the village. Manufacturing developed with the opening of the Parrett Iron Works, a series of industrial buildings next to the River Parrett. The site was originally named Carey's Mill and the adjoining bridge is called Carey's Mill Bridge, which was built of Hamstone in the eighteenth century. The Iron Works was founded in 1855 on the site of a former snuff mill. The site included a foundry with a prominent chimney, a ropewalk, workshops and several smaller buildings and cottages. The sluice which powered the waterwheel and the sluice keeper's cottage still exist.

The River Parrett is 37 miles (60 kilometres) long with its source in the hills around Chedington in Dorset. It then flows north-west through Somerset and the Somerset Levels to its mouth at Burnham-on-Sea and into the Bristol Channel.

9. MARTOCK WALK

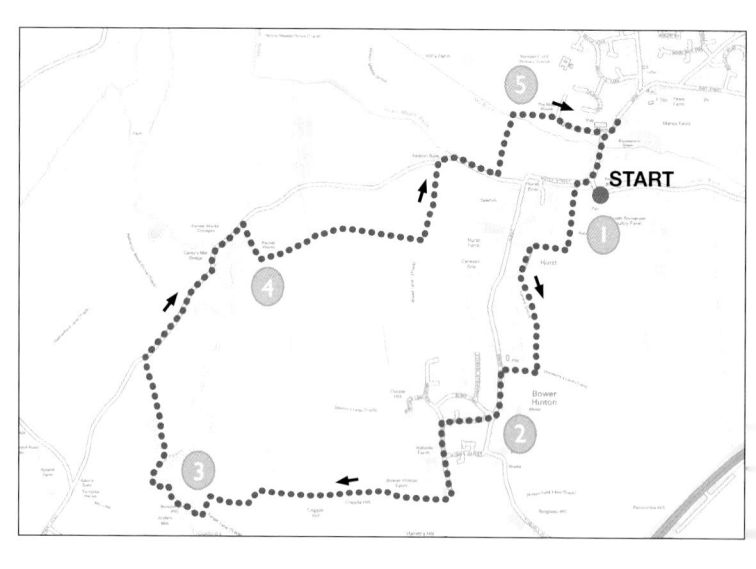

ROUTE

1. From the car park, cross the playing field towards a row of poplar trees. To the right of the trees join a gravel track across further playing fields. As the track bends right, take a track left between hedges, passing a kissing gate and continuing to a gate. Go through, turn right and continue along the track, passing houses and eventually meeting a road. Turn left and walk along the pavement to an open green on the right. Cross the road into Middle Street.

2. Walk along Middle Street to a road junction. Turn left into Back Lane, and as the road bends left continue along Back Lane past Bower Hinton Farm. Leave the road and join a track leading to a gate and stile. After 20 metres turn right and follow the track ahead at a crossroads of tracks. Continue ahead, following a farm track through several

fields over Cripple Hill. The track descends to a hedge and direction post.

3. Turn left along a field path to a stile in the hedge on your right. Cross the stile and head across the field to a gap in the hedge and a sleeper across the ditch. Turn left and follow a path between hedges, turning right and crossing a wooden bridge and then on to a metal bridge crossing the River Parrett. Keeping right, follow the path along the riverbank. Cross a stile and then leave the riverbank to follow a path towards a stile in the hedge. Cross the stile and continue down the field with the hedge on your left, passing stable buildings on your right, and go through a further gate and two metal stiles to meet the road.

4. Turn right along the road to the Parrett Works, reaching a fingerpost between a stone wall and bungalow on the right. Through the gate, follow the track to a gate, stile and hedge. Take the small gate left and follow the path between fences to a further gate, and then along the field path to a gate and bridge. Keep left to a small gate, and then on to a further gate and track. Turn left and follow the track to a road.

5. Turn right along the road until you reach a fingerpost and metal bridge on your left. Walk across a field to a gate opposite, then turn right and follow the path to a metal bridge. Cross the bridge and, keeping right, follow the edge of the field towards All Saints Church and field gate. Turn right and follow Pound Lane with the churchyard wall on your left to reach the village. To return to the car park, turn right, follow the road to the junction and cross into Stoke Lane. Martock Recreation Ground is on your right.

10. WOOKEY HOLE

THE ESSENTIALS

Distance: 6 miles (10 km)

Route: Medium; undulating paths, with steep climbs. Four stiles

Time: Approx. 3 hours

Terrain: Tracks and field paths; may be muddy

Starting Point: Market Place, Wells. **Grid ref** ST 551 495; postcode BA5 2RF

Parking: Several car parks in the city

Food and Toilets: Various restaurants and cafés in the city. Public toilets on Union Street and Market Place

Maps: OS Explorer 141 (Cheddar Gorge and Mendip Hills West); **OS Landranger** 182 (Weston-super-Mare) or 183 (Yeovil and Frome)

INTRODUCTION

This walk starts from the centre of the city of Wells and takes you through the town and out into the countryside of the Mendip Hills. The circular route takes you up onto the hills, where there are magnificent views of the Somerset Levels, Glastonbury Tor and the Quantocks in the distance. The route then takes you through Ebbor Gorge Nature Reserve and down into the village of Wookey Hole, famous for the Wookey Hole Caves.

Wells is the smallest city in England and has a magnificent cathedral. The wells which gave the city its name are located within the grounds of the Bishop's Palace, which is still the residence of the Bishop of Bath and Wells. The moated palace dates from the early thirteenth century when Bishop Jocelin

Trotman, the first to hold the title of Bishop of Bath and Wells, received a crown licence to build a residence and deer park on land to the south of the Cathedral of St Andrew.

The Mendip Hills stretch from Frome in the east of Somerset to Weston-super-Mare in the west. They are made of carboniferous limestone which is porous and allows water to percolate through the rock, and over millions of years caves have been formed underground. The most well-known of these are the Cheddar Caves and Wookey Hole.

Wookey Hole has been a source of wonder to visitors since Roman times. Carved under the beautiful Mendip Hills by the River Axe, the first known record of a cave here is from the third century AD. The caves have attracted visitors for many centuries but it is only since 1927, when electricity was introduced and stairways built, that they have been open to visitors. There are twenty-five explored caverns, with the exploration and discovery of new caverns still taking place. The mill at Wookey Hole has long been part of the village. Originally a corn mill and then a cloth mill, it has also been a paper mill. The mill and the caves are open to the public.

10. WOOKEY HOLE WALK

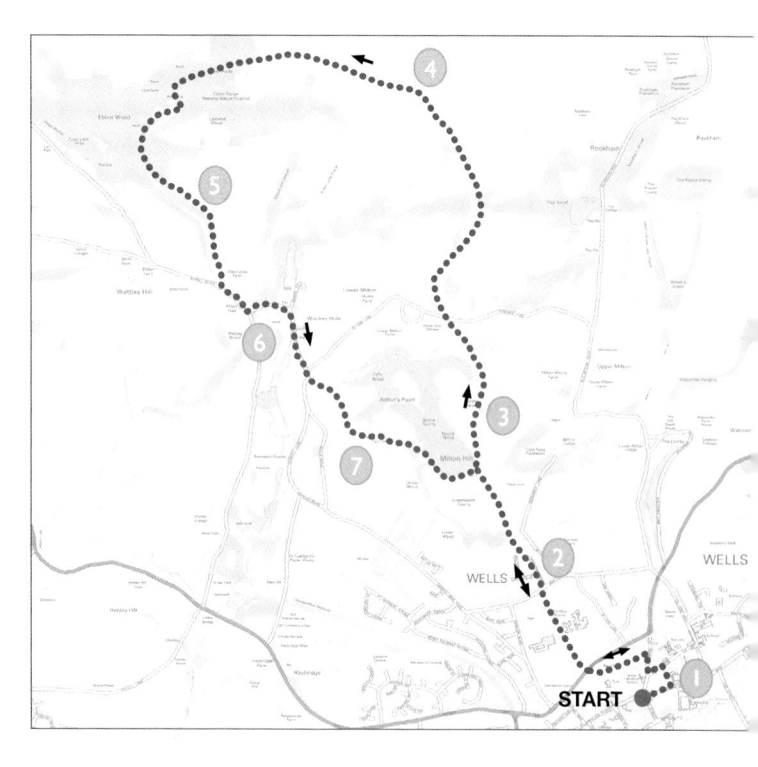

ROUTE

1. Leave the Market Place and turn right into Sadler Street to reach New Street. Turn right and take the left-hand footpath to a West Mendip Way marker post, where you turn left. Bear right, then turn left into Lovers Walk and continue across the footbridge to enter the grounds of Wells Blue School. Continue through the grounds, exit by some buildings, and continue along a tarmac path through a field to a road.

2. Cross the road to a narrow lane between houses. Climb steadily to another road; cross to rejoin the footpath,

BRADWELL'S POCKET WALKING GUIDE

continue and cross a further road. Continue on through a kissing gate to reach a waymark stating "Wookey Hole 1.5 miles". Join a minor road and follow it left.

3. Ignoring any left or right turns, continue on a grassy track to a kissing gate and field gate. Go through, bear right across a field to a kissing gate on the left of a farmhouse leading to another field, where you go downhill to cross a stream and pass through a further kissing gate. Follow the path up to the top of the ridge and then down, bearing right to another kissing gate. Continue across the field to a wooden stile in the top left-hand corner, leading onto a minor road (Milton Lane).

4. Turn left on the road, and almost immediately take the second gate on the right (opposite Lower Milton Farm Cottages). Follow a track up to a further gate. Climbing steadily, follow the track through a further gate until you reach a stile/metal gate with waymark signs. Enter a wood and continue along the track to a further gate. The track bears right and becomes more of a path leading to a further stile/gate.

5. Climb over the stile; the path now disappears. Walk up the field and look for a stile/gate in the hedge on your left on the brow of the hill. Cross the stile and continue straight ahead, following the line of the hedge to a further stile (ignore the metal stile on the right). After crossing the stile you will see a gate ahead with a waymark to the left. Bearing left, walk towards the fence. Continue left with the fence on your right, downhill to a wooden signpost with a gate and stile and the path entering Ebbor Gorge Nature Reserve. Follow the track down to a further stile, onto a stony track through woodland. At a crossing of tracks continue ahead until you see a "Cliff Edge" caution sign; take time here to enjoy the spectacular view from Ebbor Slaits rock.

continued on page 48

10. WOOKEY HOLE WALK

6. Leave Ebbor Slaits by retracing your steps, taking the first track to the right, following the "West Mendip Way" sign to the right down a footpath with numerous steps to reach a wide track at the foot of the gorge. Turn left (waymarked "Wookey Hole") and continue along the track to reach a gate/stile and information board. Cross over the stile and continue along the valley to a kissing gate and road. You are now in Wookey Hole village. Turn left on the road and continue to reach the centre of the village and the entrance to the Wookey Hole Caves and Paper Mill.

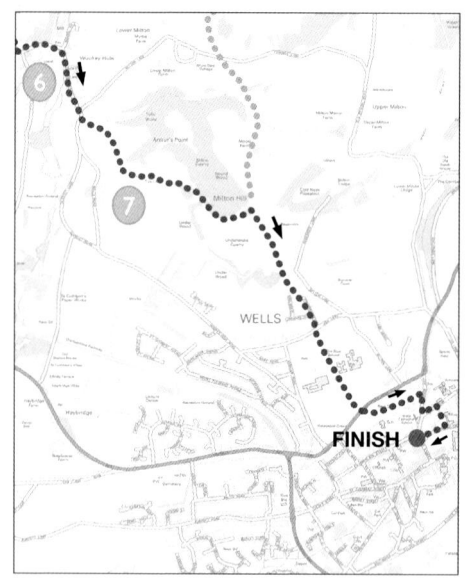

7. Continue along the road, passing the Wookey Hole Inn and ignoring the first turning on the left (Milton Lane). Continue ahead to find a kissing gate into a field on the left by a waymark. Go through the gate and follow the path to a further kissing gate, and then along a narrow path to another kissing gate. This gate leads to a minor road; turn left and continue uphill along the road to a metal gate and kissing gate. Turn right and follow the lane to a junction, then turn right. You are on the same path as your outward route. Go back through the school, over the road bridge and back to the Market Place.